A Guide for Using

Bridge to Terabithia

in the Classroom

Based on the novel written by Katherine Paterson

Written by **John and Patty Carratello**
Illustrated by **Sue Fullam**

Teacher Created Materials, Inc.
6421 Industry Way
Westminster, CA 92683
www.teachercreated.com
©1991 Teacher Created Materials, Inc.
Reprinted, 2001, a
Made in U.S.A.
ISBN-1-55734-401-9

Table of Contents

Introduction

A good book can touch our lives like a good friend. Within its pages are words and characters that can inspire us to achieve our highest ideals. We can turn to it for companionship, recreation, comfort, and guidance. It also gives us a cherished story to hold in our hearts forever.

In *Literature Units,* great care has been taken to select books that are sure to become good friends!

Teachers who use this literature unit will find the following features to supplement their own valuable ideas.

- Sample Lesson Plans

- Pre-reading Activities

- A Biographical Sketch and Picture of the Author

- A Book Summary

- Vocabulary Lists and Suggested Vocabulary Activities

- Chapters grouped for study, with each section including:

    – *quizzes*

    – *hands-on projects*

    – *cooperative learning activities*

    – *cross-curriculum connections*

    – *extensions into the reader's own life*

- Post-reading Activities

- Book Report Ideas

- Research Ideas

- A Culminating Activity

- Three Different Options for Unit Tests

- Bibliography

- Answer Key

We are confident that this unit will be a valuable addition to your planning, and hope that as you use our ideas, your students will increase the circle of "friends" that they have in books!

Sample Lesson Plan

Each of the lessons suggested below can take from one to several days to complete.

LESSON 1
- Introduce and complete some or all of the pre-reading activities found on page 5.
- Read "About the Author" with your students. (page 6)
- Read the book summary with your students. (page 7)
- Introduce the vocabulary list for SECTION 1. (page 8) Ask students to find all possible definitions for these words.

LESSON 2
- Read Chapters 1 and 2. As you read, place the vocabulary words in the context of the story and discuss their meanings.
- Play a vocabulary game. (page 9)
- Learn and practice running techniques. (page 11)
- Introduce similes and play a simile partner game. (page 12)
- Discuss the book in terms of physical education. (page 13)
- Begin "Reading Response Journals." (page 14)
- Administer the SECTION 1 quiz. (page 10)
- Introduce the vocabulary list for SECTION 2. (page 8) Ask students to find all possible definitions.

LESSON 3
- Read Chapters 3 and 4. Place the vocabulary words in context and discuss their meanings.
- Play a vocabulary game. (page 9)
- Stage a First Day of School Fashion Show! (page 16)
- Recognize and appreciate the differences in others. (page 17)
- Discuss the book in terms of science. (page 18)
- Ask students to assess their own value structures. (page 19)
- Administer SECTION 2 quiz. (page 15)
- Introduce the vocabulary list for SECTION 3. (page 8) Ask students to find all possible definitions.

LESSON 4
- Read Chapters 5 through 7. Place the vocabulary words in context and discuss their meanings.
- Play a vocabulary game. (page 9)
- Use paints to create scenes from the story. (page 21)
- Develop ways to turn foes to friends. (page 22)
- Discuss the book in terms of social studies. (page 23)
- Develop gift lists, and choose one gift from the list to make and give. (page 24)
- Administer SECTION 3 quiz. (page 20)

- Introduce the vocabulary list for SECTION 4. (page 8) Ask students to find all possible meanings.

LESSON 5
- Read Chapters 8 through 10. Place the vocabulary words in context and discuss their meanings.
- Play a vocabulary game. (page 9)
- Learn how to milk a cow and practice the skills if you are able! (page 26)
- Plan the perfect day. (page 27)
- Discuss the book in terms of art. (page 28)
- Discuss fears and how to face them. (page 29)
- Administer SECTION 4 quiz. (page 25)
- Introduce the vocabulary list for SECTION 5. (page 8) Ask students to find all possible meanings.

LESSON 6
- Read Chapters 11 through 13. Place the vocabulary words in context and discuss their meanings.
- Play a vocabulary game. (page 9)
- Make a wreath. (page 31)
- Plan the first day in Terabithia for May Belle and her king. (page 32)
- Discuss the book in terms of language arts. (page 33)
- Evaluate the dedication of *Bridge to Terabithia* in terms of personal meaning for the author. Develop ideas for special dedications for the students' own books. (page 34)
- Administer SECTION 5 quiz. (page 30)

LESSON 7
- Discuss any questions your students may have about the story. (page 35)
- Assign book report and research projects. (pages 36 and 37)
- Begin work on a culminating activity. (pages 38,39, 40, and 41)

LESSON 8
- Administer Unit Tests: 1,2, and/or 3. (pages 42, 43, and 44)
- Discuss the test answers and possibilities.
- Discuss the students' enjoyment of the book.
- Provide a list of related reading for your students. (page 45)

Before the Book

Before you begin reading *Bridge to Terabithia* with your students, do some pre-reading activities to stimulate interest and enhance comprehension. Here are some activities that might work well in your class.

1. Predict what the story might be about just by hearing the title.

2. Predict what the story might be about just by looking at the cover illustration.

3. Discuss other books by Katherine Paterson that students may have heard about or read.

4. Answer these questions:

   • Are you interested in:

     – stories about a boy and a girl becoming best friends?

     – stories about people who like to do things differently than others their own age?

     – stories about imaginary worlds?

     – stories about gaining strength and self-confidence with the help of a friend?

     – stories about dealing with death?

     – stories that make you laugh and cry and think?

   • Would you ever:

     – get up before you needed to just to practice running?

     – dress in something that might make others tease you?

     – defend a friend in front of many others who were ridiculing him or her?

     – stand up to a bully?

     – play tricks on other people?

     – have a teacher as a friend?

   • Have you ever enjoyed creating an imaginary world? Describe your experience in detail.

5. Work in groups or as a class to create your own story about the death of a friend.

About the Author

Katherine Paterson was born on October 31, 1932, in Qing Jang, Jiangsu, China, to George and Mary Womeldorf, who were in China as missionaries. Her father rode by donkey from village to village teaching the concepts of Christianity, and bringing food and medicine when they were needed. Katherine's first language was Chinese.

After her first five years in China, Katherine and her family began to move around. They moved more than fifteen times during the years from five to eighteen, and she was often very lonely. But in her loneliness, she found ideas for her writing. She also read many books to bring her comfort, and invented many stories to keep her entertained.

After graduation from King College in Bristol, Tennessee, she taught for one year in a rural elementary school. Katherine then went to graduate school for a Master's Degree in Christian education where a professor encouraged her to become a writer.

From 1957 to 1961, Katherine served as a missionary in Japan. This experience gave her new ways to express her ideas as well as new ideas. Many of Katherine's writings reflect her stay with the Japanese people.

In 1962, she met and married John Barstow Paterson, a Presbyterian minister. Katherine began her writing career during her pregnancy with her first son. At this time, the Patersons were also waiting for the arrival of their soon-to-be-adopted daughter from an orphanage in Hong Kong. Although the time to write had to be squeezed into a life as a wife and mother, she drew on these experiences to inspire and enrich her writing. For example, *Bridge to Terabithia*, was written for her son David after his best friend Lisa was struck and killed by lightning.

Katherine Paterson has received many awards for her writing. Two of her books, *Bridge to Terabithia* and *Jacob Have I Loved* received the Newbery Medal. *The Master Puppeteer, The Great Gilly Hopkins,* and *Come Sing, Jimmy Jo* have all won numerous awards.

Katherine Paterson offers this insight about her interest in writing for others:

"...I have learned, for all my failings and limitations, that when I am willing to give myself away in a book, readers will respond by giving themselves away as well, and the book that I labored over so long becomes in our mutual giving something far richer and more powerful than I could have ever imagined."

"Newbery Medal Acceptance," Horn Book, August, 1981

Bridge to Terabithia
by Katherine Paterson
(Harper & Row, 1987)

Jess Aarons wanted to be the fastest runner at Lark Creek Elementary School. He practiced all summer for his goal. But when school began in September and all the boys lined up to race, Leslie Burke became the new champion. She not only broke the race records, but the rules. Girls had never been allowed to race with the boys! Because now the race could be won by a girl, all the rest of the boys lost interest in racing, and Jess no longer had a chance at the goal he had worked so hard to attain. But he did find a friend that race day—Leslie.

Jess and Leslie had a very special friendship. With Leslie's expert guidance, they created a secret fantasy world called Terabithia, a world where they were King and Queen, and nothing could daunt them. The magic they created in Terabithia gave them imagination and compassion that touched their lives and reached far beyond the "castle" walls.

Jess grew because of Leslie. She was "more than his friend. She was his other, more exciting self— his way to Terabithia and all the worlds beyond." But Leslie drowned while going alone to Terabithia, and Jess found it difficult to accept her death.

Jess realized that Leslie's friendship had made him strong. To ease his pain and keep her memory alive, he did something that Leslie probably would have wanted him to do. He built a bridge over the creek that claimed her life and led his little sister, May Belle, across the bridge to be the new Queen of Terabithia.

Vocabulary Lists

On this page are vocabulary lists which correspond to each sectional grouping of chapters. Vocabulary activity ideas can be found on page 9 of this book.

SECTION 1

cagey	muddled
crouched	pandemonium
despised	plunked
endure	primly
goggle-eyed	proverbial
grit	pudgy
grits	thrashed
hypocritical	

SECTION 2

abruptly	reassessing
clabber	repulsive
consolation	retreating
conspicuous	roused
distribution	rumpus
exhilaration	sarcasm
grudgingly	siege
intoxicated	sulked
Narnia	swooshed
ominously	vigorously

SECTION 3

alcove	regicide
annoyance	reluctant
betrayed	roam
consolidated	smirked
crimson	snickered
distracted	speculation
dumbfounded	splurged
exiled	surplus
moony	tangle
obsessed	tolerated
parapets	vile
prey	

SECTION 4

canopy	muffled
clambered	obliged
complacent	prissy
conspiring	raveled
discern	repented
dread	sodden
earnest	spectacle
flank	sporadically
flounce	squinched
garbled	suppress
idly	vanquished
intently	wheedling

SECTION 5

assuring	objection
chaos	relentlessly
constricting	retrieved
cremated	riot
doused	traitorous
dredging	

Vocabulary Activity Ideas

You can help your students learn and retain the vocabulary in *Bridge to Terabithia* by providing them with interesting vocabulary activities. Here are a few ideas to try.

❏ People of all ages like to make and solve puzzles. Ask your students to make their own **Crossword Puzzles** or **Wordsearch Puzzles** using the vocabulary words from the story.

❏ Challenge your students to a **Vocabulary Bee!** This is similar to a spelling bee, but in addition to spelling each word correctly, the game participants must correctly define the words as well.

❏ Play **Vocabulary Concentration.** The goal of this game is to match vocabulary words with their definitions. Divide the class into groups of 2-5 students. Have students make two sets of cards the same size and color. On one set have them write the vocabulary words. On the second set have them write the definitions. All cards are mixed together and placed face down on a table. A player picks two cards. If the pair matches the word with its definition, the player keeps the cards and takes another turn. If the cards don't match, they are returned to their places face down on the table, and another player takes a turn. Players must concentrate to remember the locations of words and their definitions. The game continues until all matches have been made. This is an ideal activity for free exploration time.

❏ Have your students practice their writing skills by creating sentences and paragraphs in which multiple vocabulary words are used correctly. Ask them to share their **Compact Vocabulary** sentences and paragraphs with the class.

❏ Ask your students to create paragraphs which use the vocabulary words to present **History Lessons** that relate to the time period or historical events mentioned in the story.

❏ Challenge your students to use a specific vocabulary word from the story at least **10 Times In One Day.** They must keep a record of when, how, and why the word was used!

❏ As a group activity, have students work together to create an **Illustrated Dictionary** of the vocabulary words.

❏ Play **20 Clues** with the entire class. In this game, one student selects a vocabulary word and gives clues about this word, one by one, until someone in the class can guess the word.

❏ Play **Vocabulary Charades.** In this game, vocabulary words are acted out!

You probably have many more ideas to add to this list. Try them! See if experiencing vocabulary on a personal level increases your students' vocabulary interest and retention!

Quiz Time!

1. On the back of this paper, write a one paragraph summary of the major events in each chapter of this section. Then complete the rest of the questions on this page.

2. Why does Jess *have* to be the fastest runner?

   _____

   _____

3. How does May Belle feel about Jess?

   _____

   _____

4. What significant event happened in Jess's life on Monday, April 22?

   _____

   _____

   _____

5. How does Jess's father feel about his son's artistic interests and abilities?

   _____

   _____

   _____

6. Who is Miss Edmunds and why is she important to Jess?

   _____

   _____

   _____

7. Who is Miss Bessie? _____

   _____

8. Characterize Jess in one well-written sentence.

   _____

   _____

9. On the back of this paper, describe Jess's relationship with the members of his family.

10. On the back of this paper, explain how you would have reacted to a new neighbor who has just moved in and spoken to you.

The Art of Running

Running is important to Jesse Oliver Aarons, Jr. Winning a race is his ticket to the admiration of his peers and his father. He practices all summer long so that he will be able to win the first race in September during lunch recess. He does not know anything about running technique, except that runners in important races begin to run from a crouched position.

> "His straw-colored hair flapped hard against his forehead, and his arms and legs flew out every which way. He had never learned to run properly, but he was long-legged for a ten-year-old, and no one had more grit than he."
>
> *—Chapter 1*

Suppose Jess had a coach to school him in the skills of running. With his long legs and grit, do you think he could be the fastest runner in fifth grade if he mastered some running techniques?

Could you improve your running ability if you mastered some running techniques?

Run a short, timed race. Keep a record of your finishing time. Then read the running hints explained below. Practice the suggested techniques until you have mastered them. Then run the same racing distance you ran and timed before. Record your finishing time. Did the hints you followed and techniques you practiced improve your time?

- Prepare yourself for running by maintaining a positive attitude about running and your ability to run.
- Practice deep, rhythmic breathing to increase the ability of your lungs to supply your body with the oxygen it needs to run efficiently.
- Run in well-cushioned, flexible shoes and non-binding, comfortable clothing.
- Be sure you have rested and nourished your body adequately in order to have the stamina and strength to achieve your goal.
- Stretch before you run to warm up and lengthen the muscles you will use while you are running.
- Warm your body up gradually with an easy jog.
- Use the type of start that is appropriate for the type of race you are running.
- Do not make any wasted body motion. Make every movement support your run.
- When in a race, aim for a point several yards beyond the finish line, not on the finish line. Otherwise, you may slow down before you reach the line.
- Keep your body moving after you have finished a run. It is very important to cool your body down gradually.
- Keep a log of your running progress.
- Give yourself a lot of positive feedback!
- Keep in mind that running is fun!

Simile Partners

Throughout *Bridge to Terabithia*, Katherine Paterson chooses her words carefully to help the reader see and experience the events and feelings that are a part of her characters' lives. One of the literary techniques she uses is comparing one thing to another to stimulate a strong picture in the reader's mind. She does this through the use of *simile*. A *simile* is a form of figurative language that compares two things using the word "like" or "as" in the comparison.

Underline the things that are being compared in the sentences below. In class, discuss why the comparisons are effective.

> The little girl sings as sweetly as a nightingale.
> I don't know why, but he is as jumpy as a frog.
> My dog moves like a snail when I call him!

Brainstorm other simile ideas you have heard or read as a class.

Here are some examples of similes from Chapters 1 and 2 of the story. On the back of this paper, explain why the comparisons are effective.

- Momma would be mad *as flies in a fruit jar* if they woke her up at this time of day.

- He kept the knowledge of it buried inside himself *like a pirate treasure.*

- . . . he saw her *as a beautiful wild creature who had been caught for a moment in that dirty old cage of a schoolhouse*, perhaps by mistake.

- Beautiful Julia. The syllables rolled through his head *like a ripple of guitar chords.*

- He paused in midair *like a stop-action TV shot.* . . .

Working with a partner, complete the similes below in an imaginative way. After you have finished, create ten original similes of your own. Then, "perform" your similes for the class, with one partner saying the first part of the comparison and the other partner finishing it.

> Partner #1: "I'm as happy as . . ."
>
> Partner #2: " . . . a kid on a new bike!"

mad as . . .	happy as . . .	mean as . . .
clumsy as . . .	sweet as . . .	busy as . . .
smelly as . . .	mellow as . . .	nervous as . . .
crazy as . . .	fresh as . . .	smart as . . .
brave as . . .	quiet as . . .	tired as . . .
angry as . . .	sad as . . .	silly as . . .

Keep a record of other similes you find as you read *Bridge to Terabithia*. Discuss their effectiveness in class.

Physical Education

In the beginning of *Bridge to Terabithia,* several references are made to the types of games that were played at recess by the children at Lark Creek Elementary School.

"Lark Creek Elementary was short on everything, especially athletic equipment, so all the balls went to the upper grades at recess time after lunch. Even if a fifth grader started out the period with a ball, it was sure to be in the hands of a sixth or seventh grader before the hour was half over."

Because the older boys monopolized the balls, the lower-grade boys created the daily recess races. Some of the younger boys played "King of the Mountain," and the girls played hopscotch and jump rope.

What do you play at your school at recess?

_____

Do boys and girls play together at recess at your school?_____

If so, what do they play together? _____

If not, what do they play separately?

boys: _____

girls:_____

If you were a student at Lark Creek Elementary School, what games could you help organize that could be played without a ball?

_____

_____

If you were a student at Lark Creek Elementary School, what games could you help organize that could be played with boys and girls together?

_____

_____

Help organize and participate in a "Boys and Girls Together Recess Day" at your school. Your teacher will select the teams, mixing both boys and girls together on each team. Here are a few games you might want to include:

with a ball: soccer, basketball, softball, kickball, volleyball

without a ball: relay race, three-legged race, sack race, balloon toss, flying disk toss

Reading Response Journals

One great way to insure that the reading of *Bridge to Terabithia* touches each student in a personal way is to include the use of *Reading Response Journals* in your plans. In these journals, students can be encouraged to respond to the story in a number of ways. Here are a few ideas.

- Ask students to create a journal for *Bridge to Terabithia*. Initially, just have them assemble lined and un-lined three-holed paper in a brad-fastened "report cover," with a blank page for the journal's cover. As they read the story, they may draw a design on the cover that helps tell the story for them.

- Tell them that the purpose of the journal is to record their thoughts, ideas, observations, and questions as they read *Bridge to Terabithia*.

- Provide students with, or ask them to suggest, topics from the story that would stimulate writing. Here are a few examples from the chapters in SECTION 1.

    – Jess was so motivated by his goal to win the race at school that he rose early each day to practice. Have you ever practiced hard for something in which you wanted to be successful?

    – Jess seemed to get "stuck" doing all the work around the house. Do you ever feel that you do more work than your brothers or sisters?

    – Mr. Aarons seems to ignore Jess. Do you ever feel ignored? If so, how does it make you feel?

- After the reading of each chapter, students can write one or more new things they learned in the chapter.

- Ask students to draw their responses to certain events or characters in the story, using the blank pages in their journals.

- Tell students that they may use their journals to record "diary-type" responses that they may want to enter.

- Encourage students to bring their journal ideas to life! Ideas generated from their journal writing can be used to create plays, debates, stories, songs, and art displays.

Allow students time to write in their journals daily.

See the answer key for ideas for the evaluation of your students' Reading Response Journals.

Quiz Time!

1. On the back of this paper, write a one paragraph summary of the major events that happen in each of the chapters in this section. Then complete the rest of the questions on this page.

2. What sort of reaction does Leslie get as she walks into Mrs. Myers' class on the first day of school? _____

    _____

    _____

3. What is Jess looking forward to on the first day of school? _____

    _____

    _____

4. How is lunchtime racing changed because of Leslie's participation in it?

    _____

    _____

5. What finally brings Jess and Leslie together in friendship?

    _____

    _____

6. Mrs. Myers assigns her class a television viewing assignment. How does this assignment affect Leslie and her relationship with the other kids in her class? _____

    _____

    _____

7. Characterize Mrs. Myers in one well-written sentence. _____

    _____

    _____

8. Why do Leslie and Jess create Terabithia? _____

    _____

    _____

9. On the back of this page, write a few descriptive phrases about Leslie's parents.

10. On the back of this page, describe how being with Leslie in Terabithia makes Jess feel.

First Day of School Fashion Show!

It is the custom at Lark Creek Elementary School to dress your best on the first day of school. Therefore, it comes as no surprise that Leslie Burke makes quite an impression as she arrives in Mrs. Myers' classroom in September.

> "Leslie was still dressed in the faded cutoffs and the blue undershirt. She had sneakers on her feet but no socks. Surprise swooshed up from the class like steam from a released radiator cap. They were all sitting there primly dressed in their spring Sunday best. Even Jess wore his one pair of corduroys and an ironed shirt."

Stage a "First Day of School" Fashion Show!

This activity should be done after students have completed their reading of Chapter 3. Have students pretend it is the first day of school. Ask them to dress in clothes that best reflect their personalities. If your school has a specific dress code, be sure students stay within the guidelines.

Discuss these questions in your class:

- What is the custom at your school? Does everyone dress up in their best clothes on the first day of school, or do people dress in what makes them feel most comfortable?

- Does your school have any kind of a dress code that governs what can be worn to school?

- Do you like to dress up for school? Do your friends like to dress up? Is it practical to dress up for school?

- Are there any people in your school who are treated differently because of the clothes they wear?

- Would Leslie Burke receive a "swoosh of surprise" from the students in your classroom if she came in faded cutoffs and a blue undershirt on the first day?

- Would you ridicule her, support her, or ignore her?

Being Different

Leslie Burke is ridiculed because she is different. The girls make fun of the way she dresses, the way she acts, the food she eats, and what she does or does not have at home. Leslie's feelings are hurt considerably because of their insensitivity.

Feeling good about ourselves has a lot to do with what others say and think about us. It matters what others perceive us to be. All of us need to remember that we help to play a part in the development of a positive self-image in the people whose lives we touch every day. We must be sensitive to the feelings of others and reassure those around us that being different is acceptable, and desirable! All people are different in some way. The differences are what make our world a more interesting place. Can you imagine a world in which all people had the same color of skin, hair, and eyes, were the same height and weight, liked to eat the same kinds of foods, and had the same hobbies and jobs? Differences enrich our lives, and help make each day full of surprises!

In groups of three or four, list all the differences you can find among the people in your group. After you have completed your list, discuss how each of these differences can enrich your lives.

Here are some categories to help you get started.

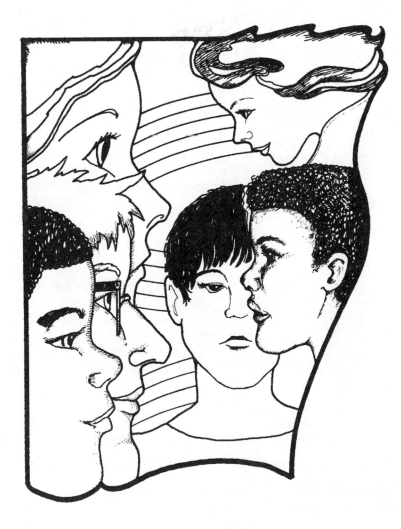

- physical characteristics
    - skin color
    - eye color
    - hair length and color
    - height and weight
    - mannerisms
- abilities
- individual preferences
- home and neighborhood experiences
- ethnic background
- religious training
- cultural background
- family standards
- family size
- allergies
- possessions
- parents' jobs
- nearness of relatives
- friendships
- fears
- hobbies
- . . . and more!

Science

SAVE THE WHALES . . . OR SOMETHING ELSE!

The Burkes are a family who keep abreast of ecological issues. They talk about "how to save the timber wolves or redwoods or singing whales" and other such topics.

For this science-related activity, you will work in groups to create a campaign that explains and supports an ecological issue.

Here are just a few topics you may want to explore:

- Saving animals that are facing extinction, such as certain species of whales, harp seals, timber wolves, elephants, and tigers
- Saving the vanishing rainforest, redwoods, and other non-renewable plant life
- Limiting the causes of acid rain
- Closing the hole in the ozone layer
- Saving streams, oceans, and other water sources
- Recycling
- Removing toxic waste properly
- Eliminating litter
- Planting trees
- Understanding the greenhouse effect and working to bring global warming under control

Work as a class to brainstorm more topic ideas. After you and your group have chosen the topic which most interests you, begin to plan your campaign. In your campaign you will:

- Research the issue you have chosen in at least three different sources. (See *Bibliography* on page 45 for suggestions.)
- Write for more information on the subject you have chosen. (Many addresses are listed in *50 Simple Things Kids Can Do to Save the Earth. See Bibliography,* page 45.)
- Interview at least one person who is knowledgeable in the field you have chosen.
- Prepare a written report on what you have discovered through your research.
- Create an interesting visual display to support your research.
- Prepare a simple handbook that can teach others about the subject. Illustrations should be included.
- Plan and present a "commercial" designed to make others want to support your cause.
- Share what you have learned with the class in an interesting manner.
- Pool your information with the information of others in your class to enlighten others in your school or community about the issues that concern you and your classmates.

Reassess Your Value Structure

The Burkes moved from the suburban city of Arlington to the old farm in the country because they wanted to "reassess their value structure." Leslie's parents decided that money and success were becoming too important to them, and they wanted to live in a place where they could think about what was really important in their lives.

Have you ever thought about what is really important in your life? Are there things that are more important than others, such as television, a bicycle, clothing, or a special toy? Are there people that are more important than others, such as a parent, a brother or sister, a special friend, or a teacher? Are there values that are more important than others for your life, such as honesty, wealth, happiness, security, good health, or popularity?

Make a list of five things, people, and values that are important in your life and rank them in their order of importance to you.

Important Things	**Important People**
1. _____	1. _____
2. _____	2. _____
3. _____	3. _____
4. _____	4. _____
5. _____	5. _____

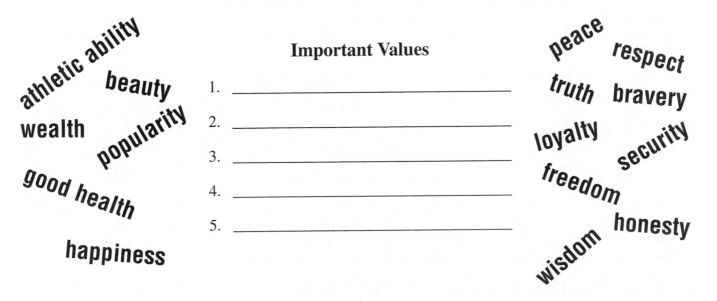

athletic ability　beauty　wealth　popularity　good health　happiness

Important Values

1. _____
2. _____
3. _____
4. _____
5. _____

peace　respect　truth　bravery　loyalty　security　freedom　wisdom　honesty

Brainstorm with your class for other values that are important to add to your list of possibilities.

Quiz Time!

1. On the back of this paper, write a one paragraph summary of the major events that happen in each of the chapters of this section. Then complete the rest of the questions on this page.

2. What does May Belle have on the bus that she loses to the bullying of Janice Avery?

    _____

    _____

3. Describe how Jess and Leslie get revenge on Janice Avery.

    _____

    _____

    _____

4. On the back of this paper, compare and contrast the relationships Jess has with his sisters.

5. Why does Jess give Leslie a puppy? _____

    _____

    _____

6. Describe the relationship Jess has with his father in one well-written sentence.

    _____

    _____

    _____

7. Describe the relationship Leslie has with her father in one well-written sentence.

    _____

    _____

    _____

8. How do Jess and Leslie feel about helping Leslie's father fix up the house?

    _____

    _____

    _____

9. On the back of this paper, explain what you might have done had you found Janice Avery crying in a private spot. Keep in mind that she has never been nice to you and, on several occasions, has been really cruel to you and your friends.

10. Who discovers Terabithia by following Jess and Leslie there?

    _____

A Set of Paints

For Christmas, Leslie gives Jess "a box of watercolors with twenty-four tubes of color and three brushes and a pad of heavy art paper." Jess is delighted with his gift. He has imagined so many pictures that could be painted with just such a set. Perhaps now he can paint one of those pictures.

In the frame below use watercolors to paint one of the pictures Jess wants to paint: the world of Terabithia; " . . . a whale shimmering white against the dark water"; a ghost coming out of the fog.

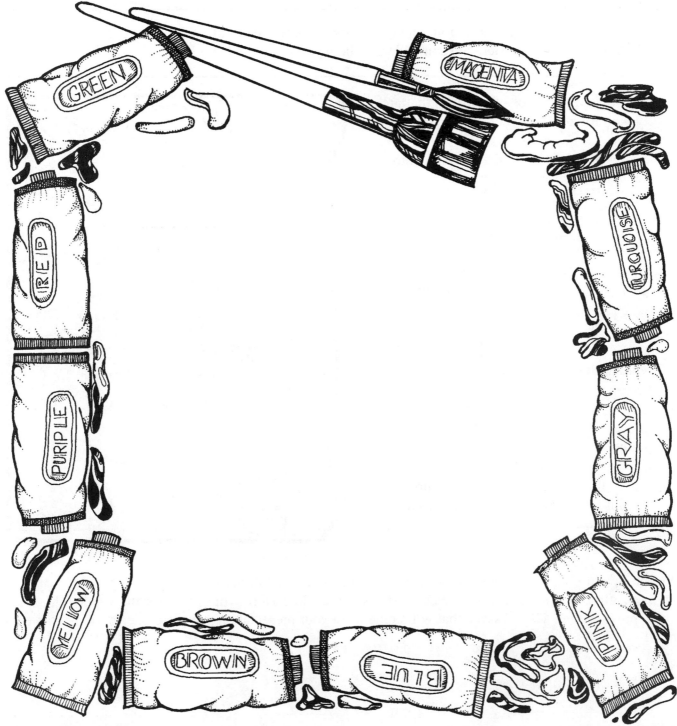

From Foe to Friend

The peace and security of Terabithia were constantly threatened by the imaginary giants who stalked the kingdom. It was all Jess and Leslie could do to keep their Terabithians safe from harm. But they knew there was also a very real giant in their lives, and her name was Janice Avery.

In Chapter 5, Janice Avery was their arch enemy, one on whom they had sworn revenge to right the wrong done to May Belle and her precious Twinkies. But by the end of Chapter 7, Leslie considered her to be half of a friend. What caused this shift from foe to friend? Discuss your answers in class.

Working in groups of two to four, create a story that dramatizes a transition in relationships from foes to friends. Here are some ideas to help you get started.

- Brainstorm the types of conflicts that are typical for students your age.

- Select one or more of these conflicts to write into a script.

- Assign parts and practice the conflict or conflicts chosen by your group.

- Brainstorm ways in which people your age can see someone they do not like in a new and positive way.

- Select one of these ways to write into your script.

- Rehearse this new scene with the same players who were used in the conflict scene.

- Put it all together and perform your "From Foe to Friend" drama for your classmates.

The groups in your classroom may want to perform some or all of these "From Foe to Friend" dramatizations for other classes as well. Perhaps you could perform your plays for the whole school or a parents' meeting. The message that will come from your presentation is a good one for all people to hear!

Social Studies

As you read *Bridge to Terabithia,* you will notice many differences between Jess and Leslie's parents. Use the chart on this page to record these differences that are described in the story.

DIFFERENCES BETWEEN THE AARONSES AND THE BURKES	
Mrs. Aarons	**Mrs. Burke**
Mr. Aarons	**Mr. Burke**

As an extension of this activity, use the back of this paper to compare your mother to Mrs. Aarons and Mrs. Burke, and your father to Mr. Aarons and Mr. Burke. Then answer the questions below.

- Do you think Jess could live easily with the Burkes? Why?

- Do you think Leslie could live easily with the Aaronses? Why?

- Would you prefer living at the Aaronses' home or the Burkes' home? Why?

- Are your parents more like the Aaronses or the Burkes? In what ways?

- Which set of parents do you think is most typical of the parents of most of the people you know? Aaronses, Burkes, or yours?

- Which set of parents do you think is typical of parents throughout the world? Why?

Gifts

In *Bridge to Terabithia*, the coming of Christmas meant the giving of gifts. Jess would be able to buy something for his family using the money his father gave him, but he did not have enough money to buy the gift for Leslie he knew she deserved. Jess "needed to give her something as much as he needed to eat when he was hungry." When he saw the sign for free puppies, he knew he had found the perfect gift. Leslie's gift for Jess was equally as special, for she gave him the watercolors he so longed to have, as well as paintbrushes and art paper. Their gifts were given and received with love.

On the occasions that you give gifts, do you take the time to try to make your gifts as special as they can be?

What is the most special gift you ever gave someone? To whom did you give it and why was it special? How did you feel when you gave it? How did the person feel when you gave it to him or her?

If you are comfortable doing so, share your experience with the class.

On the sample chart below, you will find the names of some people to whom you might be likely to give gifts. Make a copy of this chart on a separate piece of paper, adding the names of people who are important in your life but are not represented on the chart. In the appropriate spaces, write the most special gifts you have ever given each of these people and the gifts you would most like to give them.

My Gift List		
Name of Special Person	Most Special Gift I Have Ever Given	Gift I Would Most Like to Give
Mother		
Father		

(Continue this list with names to suit your own special gift-giving.)

Choose one (or more) of the gifts from your "Gift I Would Most Like To Give" list that is reasonable for you to give. Give it to the special person on your list on a gift-giving occasion. How does giving this special gift make you feel?

Quiz Time!

1. On the back of this paper, write a one paragraph summary of the major events that happen in each of the chapters in this section. Then, complete the questions on the rest of this page.

2. Where does Leslie want to go with Jess and his family? Why?

   _____

   _____

3. How do the members of the Aarons family (other than Jess) feel about Leslie?

   _____

   _____

4. Who is P.T.? _____

5. Why is Jess afraid to go to Terabithia in the rain?

   _____

   _____

   _____

6. Describe Jess's relationship with Miss Edmunds in one well-written sentence.

   _____

   _____

   _____

7. Describe Jess's response to the National Gallery of Art in Washington, D.C. in one well-written sentence. _____

   _____

8. Why does Miss Edmunds take Jess to Washington?

   _____

   _____

   _____

9. On the back of this paper, describe how the day would have been different had Jess thought to ask Miss Edmunds if Leslie could come with them to Washington.

10. What unbelievable news does Brenda give Jess about Leslie when he arrives back from Washington?

    _____

    _____

Milking Time!

Miss Bessie plays an integral part in Jess's life. Milking her is part of a regular routine, and in this routine he can escape from the noise of his family, the pressures of the household, his fears, and his feelings of inadequacy. Miss Bessie is a patient, reliable listener, and she brings him comfort.

For many, doing a repetitive task in the presence of a loving animal has the same calming, positive effect. Do you have any particular animal-related jobs that bring you comfort? How about the daily walking of a dog, or the grooming of a horse? Do you play regularly with rats, mice, or hamsters? Do you have a daily routine of feeding and providing water for wild birds? Are you responsible for milking a cow like Jess is?

Most cows today are milked by milking machines. These machines are more cost effective than milking by hand, and the machines help keep the milk cleaner. However, there are many cows throughout the world that are still milked by hand.

For this activity, you will learn the skills necessary to milk a cow and, if a friendly, willing cow is available, practice these skills on her!

Ask a local dairy owner, manager, or worker, or another person knowledgeable about milking skills to demonstrate the proper and most effective ways to milk a cow to the students in your classroom. This lesson may be taught on a class field trip to a local dairy or family farm, or on a model in the classroom that uses a milk-filled plastic glove. If it is possible, make sure every child has the opportunity to try their hands at milking!

Here is what you need:

- a cow

- a stool

- a clean container to catch the milk

- clean hands or sterilized gloves

- a supervising adult

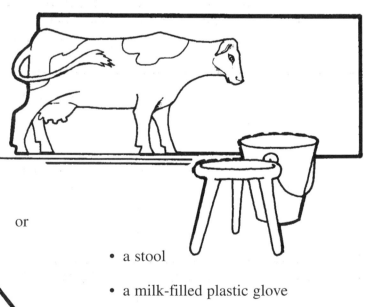

or

- a stool

- a milk-filled plastic glove

- a container to catch the milk

- clean hands

- a supervising adult

The Perfect Day

Jess Aarons had a perfect day. He went to Washington, D.C. for the very first time with someone he cared deeply about to see artwork that fascinated, inspired, and overwhelmed him. When he returned home, the "joy" was:

". . . jiggling inside of him so hard that he wouldn't have been surprised if his feet had just taken off from the ground the way they sometimes did in dreams and floated him right over the roof."

His day with Miss Edmunds had made him a truly happy boy.

* * * * *

What activities would make up a perfect day for you? Who would you be with and where would you go? Are there any similarities between Jess's perfect day and yours? Do you travel away from your home to visit museums with a teacher who understands you and appreciates who you are? Do you bicycle all day in the park with friends or visit your relatives? Maybe your idea of a perfect day is completing a special project, or sleeping in bed as long as you would like!

Work in cooperative learning groups to plan the most perfect day you could imagine. Remember that because you are working in a group, some of your individual ideas may have to be altered to meet the desires of the whole group. Work together to plan a day you can all agree is perfect!

Make your day a 24 hour one, including in it the amount of sleeping time that would be ideal. Draw an hourly view of a day on a large piece of paper as in the example below. Then fill in the perfect hourly choices, and when you have finished, share your ideas for a perfect day with your classmates. If your ideas are safe, realistic, and approved by a parent or a teacher, try to find a way to do them!

1 a.m.	2 a.m.	3 a.m.	4 a.m.	5 a.m.	6 a.m.
7 a.m.	8 a.m.	9 a.m.	10 a.m.	11 a.m.	12 a.m.
1 p.m.	2 p.m.	3 p.m.	4 p.m.	5 p.m.	6 p.m.
7 p.m.	8 p.m.	9 p.m.	10 p.m.	11 p.m.	12 p.m.

Art

Jess loves to draw. According to Miss Edmunds, he is "unusually talented" and should keep up with his drawing. In fact, it is this sensitive teacher who takes Jess to an art museum for the first time, and not just a small town one, but the National Gallery of Art in Washington, D.C.! It is an awe-inspiring experience for Jess.

> "Entering the gallery was like stepping inside the pine grove—the huge vaulted marble, the cool splash of the fountain, and the green growing all around....

> And then the pictures—room after room, floor after floor. "He was drunk with color and form and hugeness—"

Do you like to look at paintings? What kind of paintings do you enjoy? Do you know the names of any famous painters? If so, who are some of your favorite ones?

Have you ever been to an art museum? If you have not, would you like to go? If you have been to one, was your experience there anything like the experience Jess had?

Are you familiar with the types of paintings Jess saw in the National Gallery? Many famous paintings are displayed there by artists such as Cassatt, Cezanne, Degas, Van Dyck, Van Gogh, El Greco, Monet, Raphael, Rembrandt, Renoir, Rubens, Titian, and Whistler.

Work individually, in groups, or as a class to research various artists and their paintings. You may use the names listed above or choose other artists such as Michelangelo, Leonardo Da Vinci, or Picasso. (See the _Bibliography_ on page 45 for some excellent resources.) When you have completed your research, do the following things:

- Present an oral report on the painter's life.

- Show the class one or more examples of the artist's work.

- Use your own artistic skills to make a reproduction of one of your favorite paintings by the artist.

- Combine your research and artwork with the research and artwork of others in your class to make an "Art Show" in your classroom!

If possible, go to an art museum with your class!

Facing Fears

The rushing waters of the creek that marked the entrance to Terabithia brought Jess great fear. He did not want to use the rope to cross over into their kingdom, and it was only Leslie's fearlessness that prodded him on. He did not want to be afraid, but he was, and felt as if he were made with "a great piece missing."

Jess thought he might be able to overcome his fear of the rushing water if Leslie could teach him how to swim. If he could face his fear and just grab that old terror by the shoulders and shake the daylights out of it," the fear would vanish. He did not want to be paralyzed by his fear.

Do you have fears? Many people do. Some people are afraid of loud noises. Others fear snakes, spiders, and mice. Some fear high places, while others fear small, closed spaces. Some people may be so afraid of failing, they don't try. Nearly everyone has something that brings a feeling of fear.

Work together to form a class list of fears. To make sure everyone feels free to contribute ideas to the list, distribute a "FEARS FORM" like this model to each member of the class. No one will write his or her name on the form. After all forms have been completed, the teacher can collect the forms and write the ideas on the board.

As time permits, the class can discuss the fears on the list, and brainstorm for ways to help lessen or eliminate these fears. One thing that sometimes makes fears less frightening is just to talk about them. Sometimes by talking about our fears, we can start to overcome them.

FEARS FORM

Here is a list of things that I or people I know fear.

_____

_____

_____

_____

_____

_____

_____

_____

Quiz Time!

1. On the back of this page, write a one paragraph summary of the main events that happen in each of the chapters in this section. Then, complete the rest of the questions on this page.

2. What does Mr. Aarons tell Jess is the cause of Leslie's death?

   _____

   _____

3. How does Mr. Aarons show compassion for his son?

   _____

   _____

4. Why does Brenda get upset with Jess for eating so many pancakes?

   _____

   _____

5. What does Bill tell Jess about how much his friendship with Leslie meant to her?

   _____

   _____

6. Explain why Jess makes the wreath and what he does with it.

   _____

   _____

   _____

7. Describe Mrs. Myers reaction to Leslie's death on the back of this paper.

8. How has Leslie's relationship with Jess helped him grow?

   _____

   _____

9. What does Bill take with him to remind him of Leslie?

   _____

   _____

10. What opportunity does Jess give May Belle?

   _____

   _____

The Wreath

"C'mon, Prince Terrien," he said quite loudly. "We must make a funeral wreath for the queen."

He sat in the clear space between the bank and the first line of trees and bent a pine bough into a circle, tying it with a piece of wet string from the castle. And because it looked cold and green, he picked spring beauties from the forest floor and wove them among the needles.

Chapter 13

Making a tribute for Leslie in Terabithia is important for Jess. He decides to make a wreath for the queen and carries it to the sacred grove. What he does brings him peace.

Have you ever made a wreath? They are easy to make and are fun to use to decorate your house or give as gifts. Read these directions for making a simple wreath like the one Jess made for Leslie. If you enjoy making this one, look in the answer key for more wreath ideas!

Here is what you will need for the project.

- a flexible pine bough or other type of greenery (may be real or artificial)
- string
- flowers (may be real or artificial)
- florist's wire or tape

Here are the directions for the project.

1. Bend the pine bough in a circle. Be sure that the foliage is thickly and evenly distributed around the circle.

2. Tie the ends of the wreath together with a string or florist's wire.

3. Arrange flowers around the wreath, securing them with florist's wire or tape.

Terabithia Revisited

Jess has built the bridge to Terabithia and has invited May Belle to join him for the first time. He arranges flowers in her hair and leads her across the bridge. He begins to spin some of the magic around her.

> "Can't you see 'um? All the Terabithians standing on tiptoe to see you. . . . There's a rumor going around that the beautiful girl arriving today might be the queen they've been waiting for."

Do you think May Belle is really excited, invited at last to join her brother in the magic land of Terabithia?

For this activity, you will need to be divided into cooperative learning groups of three or four people. In your groups, you will work together to plan May Belle's first week in Terabithia.

You might want to include some of these ideas in your planning, as well as many ideas of your own.

- May Belle's first questions for Jess

- May Belle's first reactions to being in Terabithia

- Jess's explanation of Terabithia

- What Jess shares with his sister about Terabithia

- What Jess shares with his sister about Leslie

- When, where, and how May Belle becomes queen

- May Belle's walk to the sacred grove and her reaction to it

- Things Jess keeps the same in Terabithia

- Things Jess changes in Terabithia

- A list of things Jess and May Belle do the first week there

- Stories Jess chooses to tell her or read to her

- The level of May Belle's excitement about Terabithia

- The level of Jess's excitement about Terabithia

- The new relationship between Jess and May Belle

- The possibilities for Joyce Ann in Terabithia

After you have planned May Belle's first week in Terabithia, choose one or more of your ideas to dramatize for the class.

Language Arts

Leslie was well-suited to the imaginary world of Terabithia, and Jess was in awe of her ability to behave like a royal ruler. Her comfort with the role of nobility was evident in the manner in which she walked, planned activities, and spoke. Her speech was full of the poetic language of a true queen, and Jess tried to emulate her regal style as best he could.

Remember these royal words from the story?

"This is a time of greatest joy."

"We've been away for many years. How do you suppose the kingdom has fared in our absence?"

"We must have courage, my king. It may indeed be so."

"Thy sword, sire."

"Arise, arise, king of Terabithia, and let us proceed into our kingdom."

"I will arise when thou removes this fool dog off my gut."

"Let us go even up into the sacred grove and inquire of the Spirits what this evil might be and how we must combat it. For of a truth I perceive that this is no ordinary rain that is falling upon our kingdom."

Can you say things you normally say in a regal manner? Try to "translate" these sentences into the poetic language of Terabithia. You may work by yourself or with a partner.

1. It's time to eat.
2. This place is special.
3. It's raining.
4. You are acting silly.
5. I'm tired.
6. Let's plan a party!
7. Listen to that bird singing.
8. I missed you.
9. It's been a long time since we came here.
10. It is a secret.
11. Did you finish your homework?

12. That's ridiculous!
13. Watch out!
14. Please be quiet.
15. I can't go with you today.
16. See you tomorrow!
17. Awesome!
18. Did you hear me call you?
19. It will be dark soon.
20. What time is it?

Think of more sentences, phrases, and words you can "translate." Then perform all your "regal words" for the class!

Dedications

A dedication in a book tells readers who the author had in mind when the book was written, who served to support or inspire the author in some way, or who is very special in the author's life. For Katherine Paterson, the dedication of her book reflects all of these reasons. By reading the biographical sketch of her life on page 6, you learned that she wrote *Bridge to Terabithia* for her son David, after he experienced the death of his best friend Lisa Hill. Reread the book's dedication.

> "I wrote this book for my son David Lord Paterson, but after he read it he asked me to put Lisa's name on this page as well, and so I do. For David Paterson and Lisa Hill, *banzai*"

After reading the book, do you think this dedication is a meaningful one? Why? Do you think *Bridge to Terabithia* helped David Paterson deal with the death of his friend Lisa? Why?

_____

_____

How do you think Lisa Hill's family felt after reading *Bridge to Terabithia*?

_____

_____

Have you ever experienced the death of a friend? If you are comfortable doing so, share your experience with the class. If not, write your thoughts on a piece of paper.

_____

_____

If you have had a friend or other person who was close to you die, did reading this book help you in any way? Explain.

_____

_____

_____

Suppose someday you were to write a book that touched many, many lives. What would your book be about, and to whom would you dedicate it? Write the dedication for this book and share both the dedication and the book idea with your classmates.

_____

_____

Any Questions?

When you finished reading *Bridge to Terabithia*, did you have some questions that were left unanswered? Write some of your questions here.

_____

_____

_____

Work in groups or by yourself to prepare possible answers for some or all of the questions you have asked above and those written below. When you have finished your predictions, share your ideas with the class.

- For how long does Jess continue the fantasy of Terabithia?
- Does May Belle become the new queen?
- Is Joyce Ann invited to join her brother and sister in Terabithia?
- Do the rulers of Terabithia ever attach a new rope to the crab apple tree as a way to enter the kingdom?
- How does Terabithia change without Leslie there?
- Do Mr. and Mrs. Aarons ever find out about Terabithia?
- Does Miss Edmunds ever find out about Terabithia?
- Does Miss Edmunds continue to play a meaningful role in Jess's life?
- Are there any more trips to Washington for Jess and Miss Edmunds?
- Does Jess ever ask his father to take him to Washington with him so they can see the National Gallery and the Smithsonian together?
- Does Jess begin to share his art with his father? If he does, what is his father's reaction?
- How does Leslie's death change the relationship between Jess and his family?
- Do Jess and his father begin to spend more time together?
- Does Jess ever get a dog? If he does, what does he name the puppy?
- Do new people move into the Perkins place?
- Do Janice Avery and her buddies continue to terrorize the younger children at Lark Creek Elementary School?
- Does Janice Avery ever talk to Jess about Leslie?
- What do the kids in Mrs. Myers' class say about Leslie's death?
- What is the relationship between Jess and Mrs. Myers for the remainder of the school year?
- Do the boys at Lark Creek ever run again? Does Jess?
- Does Jess find another best friend?
- Do the Burkes ever return for a visit?
- Does Jess ever go to Arlington to visit the Burkes?
- Does Jess learn to swim and lose his fear of rushing water?
- Does the confidence Leslie helped Jess find in himself stay with him?
- Does Jess ever "pay back to the world in beauty and caring what Leslie had loaned him in vision and strength"? How?

Book Report Ideas

There are numerous ways to report on a book once you have read one.

After you have finished reading *Bridge to Terabithia*, choose one method of reporting on the book that interests you. It may be a way that your teacher suggests, an idea of your own, or one of the ways that is mentioned below.

- **See What I Read?**

  This report is a visual one. A model of a scene from the story can be created, or a likeness of one or more of the characters from the story can be drawn or sculpted.

- **Time Capsule**

  This report provides people living at a "future" time with the reasons *Bridge to Terabithia* is such an outstanding book, and gives these "future" people reasons why it should be read. Make a time capsule-type of design, and neatly print or write your reasons inside the capsule. You may wish to "bury" your capsule after you have shared it with your classmates. Perhaps one day someone will find it and read *Bridge to Terabithia* because of what you wrote!

- **Come to Life!**

  This report is one that lends itself to a group project. A size-appropriate group prepares a scene from the story for dramatization, acts it out, and relates the significance of the scene to the entire book. Costumes and props will add to the dramatization!

- **Into the Future**

  This report predicts what might happen if *Bridge to Terabithia* were to continue. It may take the form of a story in narrative or dramatic form, or a visual display.

- **A Letter to the Author**

  In this report, you can write a letter to Katherine Paterson. Tell her what you liked about *Bridge to Terabithia*, and ask her any questions you may have about the writing of the book. You might want to give her some suggestions for a sequel! After your teacher has read it, and you have made your writing the best it can be, send it to her in care of the publishing company.

- **Guess Who or What!**

  This report takes the form of several games of "Twenty Clues." The reporter gives a series of clues about a character from the story in a vague to precise, general to specific order. After all clues have been given, the identity of the mystery character must be deduced. After the character has been guessed, the same reporter presents another "Twenty Clues" about an event in the story.

- **A Character Comes to Life!**

  Suppose one of the characters in *Bridge to Terabithia* came to life and walked into your home or classroom? This report gives a view of what this character sees, hears, and feels as he or she experiences the world in which you live.

- **Sales Talk**

  This report serves as an advertisement to "sell" *Bridge to Terabithia* to one or more specific groups. You decide on the group to target and the sales pitch you will use. Include some kind of graphics in your presentation.

- **Coming Attraction!**

  Bridge to Terabithia is about to be made into a movie and you have been chosen to design the promotional poster. Include the title and author of the book, a listing of the main characters and the contemporary actors who will play them, a drawing of a scene from the book, and a paragraph synopsis of the story.

- **Literary Interview**

  This report is done in pairs. One student will pretend to be a character in the story, steeped completely in the persona of his or her character. The other student will play the role of a television or radio interviewer, trying to provide the audience with insights into the character's personality and life. It is the responsibility of the partners to create meaningful questions and appropriate responses.

Research Ideas

Describe three things you read in *Bridge to Terabithia* that you would like to learn more about.

1. _____

2. _____

3. _____

As you read *Bridge to Terabithia*, you encountered geographical locations, teaching methods, song and book titles, culturally and philosophically diverse people, coping techniques, and a variety of plants and animals. To increase your understanding of the characters and events in the story as well as more fully recognize Katherine Paterson's craft as a writer, research to find out more about these people, places, and things!

Work in groups to research one or more of the areas you named above, or the areas that are mentioned below. Share your findings with the rest of the class in any appropriate form of oral presentation.

- Washington, D.C.
- The National Gallery of Art
- The Smithsonian
- Arlington Cemetery
- The Capitol
- The White House
- Lee Mansion
- Lincoln Memorial
- Washington Monument
- watercolor
- Italian cars
- songs

    "Free To Be You and Me"
    "My Beautiful Balloon"
    "This Land Is Your Land"
    "Blowing in the Wind"

- instruments

    – guitar
    – autoharp
    – triangles
    – cymbals
    – tambourines
    – bongo drum

- scuba diving

- types of trees
    – crab apple
    – dogwood
    – redbud
    – oak
    – evergreen
    – pine
    – redwoods
- timber wolves
- whales
- dairy cows
- string quartet
- hippies
- peacenik
- book titles
    – *Hamlet*
      by William Shakespeare
    – *Moby Dick*
      by Herman Melville
    – *The Chronicles of Narnia*
      by C.S. Lewis
- clabber
- Walter Cronkite
- "Dear Abby"

Your Fantasy World

Would you like to create your own secret, magical, fantasy world such as Terabithia? For this culminating activity, you will!

Make a scrapbook of your world that includes the items on the list below. You may work by yourself or with a partner.

- Design a scrapbook cover with the name of your world done as neatly and imaginatively as you can. Include your name on the cover.

- Make a title page which explains in one well-written paragraph the reasons your fantasy world was created. Include on this page one illustration of a bit of your world.

- Write a dedication page.

- Give a brief history of your world.

- Draw a detailed map of your world. Include your entrance and exit, as well as things such as land features, where you sit most often, inspirational places, and any other areas you would like to include.

- Introduce the inhabitants of your world, real and imaginary. (See page 39.)

- Give examples of special ways of talking while in your world, or secret codes and messages that are used.

- Make a list of rules that must be followed while in your kingdom. (See page 40.)

- Determine a creed by which all who live in your kingdom must abide.

- Write a song which will serve as the anthem for your world.

- Create the story of one conflict that happens to you while in your fantasy world.

- Write a journal entry for one day in your special world. (See page 41.)

- List the supplies you will need while in your world.

- Make a bibliography of books and other reading materials that are important in your kingdom.

- Explain your part in this world.

- Predict your future in this world. Will you stay or leave? Are you and will you always be welcome? Will you share you world with others?

- Draw your favorite place in this world with which to end your scrapbook.

- Of course, you may make any other scrapbook pages which are important to you!

Your Fantasy World *(cont.)*

Complete this "meet the inhabitants" form, naming and describing the characters in your world. Then cut it out and paste the list in your scrapbook.

The ruler of _____

is _____

Here is a description of the physical appearance and personality of our ruler:

physical appearance:_____

_____

_____

_____

personality:_____

_____

_____

_____

These are the characters who uphold the good in our world, and a description of each:

_____

_____

_____

These are the characters who cause problems in our world, and a description of each: _____

_____

_____

_____

These are the people to whom the inhabitants of our kingdom will always give a special welcome:

_____

_____

Your Fantasy World *(cont.)*

Write the list of rules which govern your fantasy world. Then cut the rule page out and paste it in your scrapbook.

We, the inhabitants of the world of

_____ ,

do solemnly decree these rules to govern our kingdom:

Your Fantasy World *(cont.)*

Write a one day diary account of the things you do, the people you do them with, the problems you face, the solutions you find, the things you eat, the ways you feel, the dreams you dream, the realities you face, and anything else you may want to record while "living" in your fantasy world. Then, cut this page out and paste it in your scrapbook.

Date: _____

Unit Test

Matching: Match the names of the characters with their descriptions.

1._____ Jess   a. cow in the Aaronses' pasture

2._____ Leslie   b. sister who adores Jess

3._____ May Belle   c. teacher who encourages imagination

4._____ Ellie   d. father who talks and shares love easily with his child

5._____ Mr. Aarons   e. sister who adores clothes, not Jess

6._____ Mr. Burke   f. girl who loves to imagine

7._____ Miss Edmunds g. mean girl who shows a nice side

8._____ Miss Bessie   h. guardian of Terabithia

9._____ Janice Avery i. father who does not talk and share love easily with his child

10._____ Prince Terrien j. boy who loves to draw

True or False: Write true or false next to each statement below.

1._____ Jess needs Leslie as much as she needs him.

2._____ The Aaronses have a very close and loving relationship with their son.

3._____ The order of the Aarons children from oldest to youngest is Brenda, Ellie, Jess, May Belle, and Joyce Ann.

4._____ Leslie is able to make many friends at school.

5._____ Bill blames Jess for Leslie's death in Terabithia.

Short Answer: Provide a short answer for each of these questions.

1. Who is the only member of the Aarons family Jess feels close to? _____

2. How do Jess and Leslie cross over into Terabithia? _____

3. What do Jess and Leslie give each other for Christmas? _____

4. What person from school is both a foe and a friend for Leslie?_____

5. Who may be the new Queen of Terabithia? _____

Essay: Answer these questions on the back of this paper.

1. Describe how Jess grows because of his relationship with Leslie.

2. Explain what Jess does to "repay" Leslie for all she has done for him.

Response

Explain the meaning of each of these quotations from *Bridge to Terabithia*.

Chapter 1   *"One time last year Jesse had won. Not just the first heat but the whole shebang. Only once. But it had put into his mouth a taste for winning."*

Chapter 1   *"Jess drew the way some people drink whiskey. The peace would start at the top of his muddled brain and seep down through his tired and tensed-up body. Lord, he loved to draw."*

Chapter 2   *"Mighty late with the milking, aren't you, son ? It was the only thing his father said directly to him all evening."*

Chapter 2   *"You're the only kid in this whole durned school who's worth shooting."*

Chapter 3   *"He felt there in the teachers' room that it was the beginning to a new season in his life, and he chose to make it so."*

Chapter 4   *"He believed her because there in the shadowy light of the stronghold everything seemed possible. Between the two of them they owned the world and no enemy, Gary Fulcher, Wanda Kay Moore, Janice Avery, Jess's own fears and insufficiencies, nor any of the foes whom Leslie imagined attacking Terabithia, could ever really defeat them."*

Chapter 4   *"For the first time in his life he got up every morning with something to look forward to. Leslie was more than his friend. She was his other, more exciting self—his way to Terabithia and all the worlds beyond."*

Chapter 4   *"She stole my Twinkies!"*

Chapter 5   *". . . Meet me behind the school this afternoon after school. Do not worry about missing your bus. I want to walk home with you and talk about US . . ."*
"Maybe I got this thing for Janice like you got this thing for killer whales."

Chapter 5   *"Jess tried going to Terabithia alone, but it was no good. It needed Leslie to make the magic. He was afraid he would destroy everything by trying to force the magic on his own, when it was plain that the magic was reluctant to come for him."*

Chapter 7   *"Thanks to you, I think I now have one and one-half friends at Lark Creek School."*

Chapter 7   *They smiled at each other trying to ignore May Belle's anxious little voice. "But Leslie," she insisted. "What if you die? What's going to happen to you if you die?"*

Chapter 8   *"I'll just grab that old terror by the shoulders and shake the daylights out of it. Maybe I'll even learn scuba diving."*

Chapter 10   *"She loved you; you know." He could tell from Bill's voice that he was crying. "She told me once that if it weren't for you. . ." His voice broke completely. "Thank you," he said a moment later. "Thank you for being such a wonderful friend to her."*

Chapter 12   *"It—it—we—I never had such a student. In all my years of teaching. I shall always be grateful—"*

Chapter 13   *"It was Leslie who had taken him from the cow pasture into Terabithia and turned him into a king."*

Chapter 13   *"As for the terrors ahead—for he did not fool himself that they were all behind him—well, you just have to stand up to your fear and not let it squeeze you white. Right, Leslie?"*

Chapter 13   *"Shh, yes. There's a rumor going around that the beautiful girl arriving today might be the queen they've been waiting for."*

Teacher Note: Choose an appropriate number of quotes for your students.

Conversations

Work in size-appropriate groups to write and perform the conversations that might have occurred in each of the following situations.

- Jess and May Belle talk about why he likes to run. (2 people)

- Miss Bessie tells Jess what she thinks of his habit of running in her pasture. (2 people)

- Jess talks to his father about why he likes to draw. His mother and sisters listen in. (2 or more people)

- Miss Edmunds talks to Mr. and Mrs. Aarons about Jess's aptitude for art. (3 people)

- In Mrs. Myers' class on the first day of school, Wanda Kay Moore and several other girls in the class talk about Leslie's clothes. Jess, Leslie, and Mrs. Myers hear them. (5 or more people)

- Gary Fulcher, Greg Williams, Jimmy Mitchell, Clyde Deal, and Jess get into a heated discussion about a girl entering the lunchtime recess race. Leslie adds her comments as well. (6 people)

- Jess makes a special point of taking Leslie to meet Miss Edmunds after their Friday music lesson. (3 people)

- Leslie explains to the fifth grade why her parents have chosen to eliminate television from their home. Several students and Mrs. Myers respond. (4 or more people)

- Leslie explains the concept of Terabithia to Jess. (2 people)

- Janice Avery, Wilma Dean, and Bobby Sue Henshaw terrorize a small group of primary girls, one of whom is May Belle. (4 or more people)

- Billy Morris tells Willard Hughes about the letter Janice has been showing to the girls in the seventh grade. (2 people)

- Leslie talks to her parents about how special Jess is. (3 people)

- Jess talks to his parents about how special Leslie is. (3 people)

- Bill and Judy Burke talk to Jess about the things they do and are interested in doing. (3 people)

- Leslie finds out from Janice Avery what has made her cry in the bathroom. (2 people)

- Jess and Leslie have a conversation in Terabithia in the language that is most fitting for them to speak. (2people)

- Miss Edmunds and Jess invite Leslie to join them on the trip to Washington, D.C. They go. (3 people)

- Jess's family tries their best to comfort him after Leslie's death. (7 people)

- Jess and the Burkes comfort each other after Leslie's death. (3 people)

- Jess tells May Belle about Terabithia. (2 people)

- May Belle tells Joyce Ann about Terabithia. (2 people)

- Jess has a one-sided conversation with Leslie after her death. He tells her what she has meant to him. (1 person)

Write and perform one of your own conversation ideas for the characters from *Bridge to Terabithia*.

Bibliography

Alexander, Sue. *Lila on the Landing.* (Clarion, 1987)

Banks, Lynne Reid. *The Indian in the Cupboard.* (Doubleday, 1980) This book's sequels, *The Return of the Indian* and *The Secret of the Indian* are also excellent related-reading experiences.

Bauer, Marion Dane. *On My Honor.* (Dell, 1986)

Brown, Joseph E. *Rescue From Extinction.* (Dodd, Mead & Company, 1981)

Bulla, Clyde Robert. *The Chalk Box Kid.* (Random House, 1987)

Burnett, Frances Hodgson. *The Secret Garden.* (Dell, 1987)

Chase, Alice Elizabeth. *Famous Paintings: An Introduction to Art for Young People.* (Platt and Munk, 1951)

Cooper, Kenneth H. *Aerobics.* (M. Evans, 1968)

Cutler, Katherine N. *From Petals to Pinecones.* (Lothrop, Lee & Shepard, 1969)

Fanning, Tony and Robbie. *Keep Running* (Sovereign, 1978)

Javna, John. *50 Simple Things Kids Can Do to Save the Earth .* (The Earth Works Group, 1990)

Lewis, C.S. *The Chronides of Narnia.* (Collier, 1970)

McGrath, Susan. *Saving Our Animal Friends.* (National Geographic Society, 1986)

McMane, Fred. *Track & Field Basics.* (Prentice-Hall, 1983)

Miles, Betty. *Save the Earth! An Ecology Handbook for Kids.* (Knopf, 1974)

Paterson, Katherine.
>   *Angels and Other Strangers: Family Christmas Stories.* (Crowell, 1979)
>   *Bridge to Terablthia.* (Harper & Row, 1987)
>   *Come Sing, Jimmy Jo.* (Dutton, 1985)
>   *The Crane Wife.* (Morrow, 1981)
>   *Gates of Excellence: On Reading and Writing Books for Children* (adult). (Elsevier/Nelson, 1981)
>   *The Great Gilly Hopkins.* (Crowell, 1978)
>   *Jacob I Have Loved.* (Avon, 1981)
>   *The Master Puppeteer.* (Crowell, 1976)
>   *Of Nightingales That Weep.* (Crowell, 1974)
>   *Park's Quest.* (Dutton, 1988)
>   *The Sign of the Chrysanthemum.* (Crowell, 1973)
>   *The Tongue-Cut Sparrow.* (Dutton, 1987)

Raboff, Ernest. *Art for Children.* (Harper&Row, 1987) (There are numerous titles in this series, among them are *Vincent Van Gogh, Rembrandt, Michelangelo, Leonardo Da Vinci,* and *Pablo Picasso,* to name a few.)

Rice, Melanie and Chris. *I Like Painting.* (Warwick, 1989)

Rivers, Beverly, editor. *Traditional American Crafts.* (Meredith Corporation, 1988)

Ruskin, Ariane. *The Pantheon Story of Art.* (Pantheon, 1964)

Sachs, Marilyn. *The Bears' House.* (Avon, 1989)

Smith, Doris Buchanan. *A Taste of Blackberries.* (Harper & Row, 1988)

Snyder, Zilpha Keatley. *The Egypt Game.* (Dell, 1986)

Ventura, Piero. *Great Painters.* (G.P. Putnam's Sons, 1984)

Walker, John. *National Gallery of Art, Washington, D.C..* (Harry N. Abrams, no date given)

Winthrop, Elizabeth. *The Castle in the Attic.* (Bantam, 1986)

Zaidenberg, Arthur. *How to Paint with Water Colors: A Book for Beginners.* (Vanguard Press, 1968)

Answer Key

Page 10

1. Accept appropriate responses.
2. Jess has to be the fastest runner because winning would make him special, if only for a day.
3. May Belle worships Jess.
4. He won the race at school and felt special all that day.
5. Mr. Aarons doesn't want Jess to draw. He thinks that drawing is feminine.
6. Miss Edmunds is the Friday music teacher, and believes in and encourages Jess. He loves her.
7. Miss Bessie is the Aarons family cow.
8. Accept reasonable answers.
9. Discuss descriptions of family relationships in class. Accept reasonable answers.

Page 14

Explain to the students that their Reading Response Journals can be evaluated in a number of ways. Here are a few ideas.

• Personal reflections will be read by the teacher, but no corrections or letter grades will be assigned. Credit is given for effort, and all students who sincerely try will be awarded credit. If a "grade" is desired for this type of entry, you could grade according to the number of journal entries for the number of journal assignments. For example, if five journal assignments were made and the student conscientiously completes all five, then he or she should receive an "A."

• Non-judgmental teacher responses should be made as you read the journals to let the students know that you are reading and enjoying their journals. Here are some types of responses that will please your journal writers and encourage them to write more.

    – "You have really found what's important in the story!"

    – "WOW! This is interesting stuff!"

    – "You write so clearly, I almost feel as if I am there!"

    – "You seem to be able to learn from this book and apply what you learn to your life!"

    – "If you feel comfortable doing so, I'd like you to share your idea with the class. They will enjoy what you've written!"

• If you would like to grade something for form and content, ask the students to select one of their entries and "polish it" according to the writing process.

Page 15

1. Accept appropriate responses.
2. The kids are "rudely" amazed at Leslie's "careless" dress.
3. Jess is looking forward to running and winning the race.
4. Because Leslie always wins, the boys lose interest in racing.
5. Jess and Leslie are brought together while singing with Miss Edmunds.
6. Leslie has no television set, which brings her more ridicule.
7. Accept appropriate responses.
8. It is a secret place, just for their friendship.
9. Ideas: writers, political activists, long haired adults, owners of an Italian car, musical, ecologically and environmentally-oriented, etc.
10. Ideas: excited, good, exhilarated, comfortable, special, etc.

Page 20

1. Accept appropriate responses.
2. Janice steals May Belle's Twinkies.
3. They write the "false" love note and embarrass her.
4. May Belle is very special to Jess. She idolizes him and he appreciates her good nature. He loves her more than his other sisters. Joyce Ann is a nuisance, crying when she doesn't get her way, and manipulating his mother to get Jess in trouble. He does like her, but she is just a bit young for the "comradery" he feels with May Belle. Ellie and Brenda are very self-centered, and tease Jess constantly. Their selfishness amazes him, and they do not appear to like him at all. Jess seems to feel no special warmth for them.

Answer Key *(cont.)*

5. The puppy is free and Jess has no money. Besides, he really wants to give Leslie a gift that is special and makes him proud to give. The puppy satisfies both these needs.

6. Accept appropriate responses.

7. Accept appropriate responses.

8. They both enjoy it. Leslie enjoys being needed by her father and Jess enjoys their company and being helpful.

9. Accept all clearly explained responses.

10. May Belle finds Terabithia.

Page 25

1. Accept appropriate responses.

2. She goes to church with the Aarons to have a new experience.

3. They don't particularly like her. They think she is strange and boyish, and not a suitable companion for Jess. May Belle and Joyce Ann like her.

4. P.T. is Leslie's dog, Prince Terrien.

5. The rushing water scares him.

6. Accept appropriate responses.

7. Accept appropriate responses.

8. Miss Edmunds takes Jess to Washington to give him a taste of art and culture.

9. Accept reasonable responses.

10. Brenda tells him that Leslie is dead.

Page 30

1. Accept appropriate responses.

2. The rope broke while she was swinging to Terabithia and she probably hit her head on a rock.

3. Mr. Aarons is gentle with Jess and holds him when he needs to be held. He shows his son he cares.

4. Brenda thinks Jess shouldn't be eating so much. After all, his best friend has just died.

5. Leslie loved Jess, and the friendship between them made her stay at the old farm a positive experience rather than a negative one.

6. Jess makes a wreath as an offering for a dear friend. He takes the funeral wreath to the sacred grove, giving it to the "spirits" in her memory.

7. Mrs. Myers is deeply touched by Leslie's death. Leslie was very special to Mrs. Myers as well. She showed Jess great empathy.

8. Leslie "had taken him from the cow pasture into Terabithia and turned him into a king." Accept appropriate responses.

9. Bill takes Prince Terrien.

10. Jess gives May Belle the chance to be the new queen of Terabithia.

Page 31

• To preserve flowers for a wreath:

Air Drying

Most flowers, grasses, herbs, and weeds can be air dried. Air drying is cheap, simple, and effective! All you need is a warm, dry, clean, airy, and dark place.

Cut the flowers just before they are in full bloom and remove the leaves. Group flower families together, using a string or rubber band to tie their stems together. Be sure not to smash the blossoms tightly together because air must be able to circulate around the petals to dry the blossoms thoroughly in their original shape.

Hang the flower groupings upside-down, suspended from a nail, wire, string, or coat hanger. They will be dry in three to five weeks.

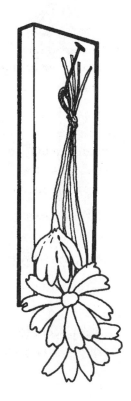

Answer Key *(cont.)*

Sand Drying

To preserve flowers, grasses, herbs, and weeds with sand, place them on an inch or two of fine, clean, dry sand in a container such as a shoebox. Then cover them with more fine, clean, dry sand. The container is left open for three to five weeks to allow for the evaporation of the water in the plants.

• To make a wreath base:

You can, as Jess did, make a wreath out of a bough of pine or other pliable foliage, such as willow, privet, or forsythia. You may also make (or purchase) a straw, wire, moss, or fabric wreath for your base.

• Here are a few pictures of wreaths you can make.

Pages 38 to 41

Create a classroom display of these culminating activities.

Page 42

Matching

1)j 2)f 3)b 4)e 5)i 6)d 7)c 8)a 9)g 10)h

True or False

1. True

2. False—Mrs. Aarons is always yelling at Jess and calling him useless. Mr. Aarons seems to ignore him.

3. False—Ellie is older than Brenda.

4. False—Leslie only manages to make two friends at school besides Mrs. Meyers and May Belle: Jess and Janice Avery.

5. False—He is deeply grateful to Jess for his friendship with his daughter. He has only love for Jess.

Short Answer

1. May Belle

2. by swinging on the rope tied to the crab apple tree

3. a puppy, and paper and a paint set

4. Janice Avery

5. May Belle

Essay

1. Accept appropriate responses. Answers should reflect the great self-confidence, creativity, and caring Jess had received in his friendship with Leslie, and/or the idea that Leslie had "taken him from the cow pasture into Terabithia and turned him into a king."

2. Accept appropriate responses. Included in answers could be the idea that Jess needed to spread the joy of Terabithia and the creativity it inspired to others, especially May Belle and Joyce Ann.

Page 43

Accept all reasonable and well-supported answers.

Page 44

Perform the conversations in class. Ask students to respond to the conversations in several different ways, such as, "Are the conversations realistic?" or, "Are the words the characters say in keeping with their personalities?"